# BIRDS OF PREY

## Explore the Fascinating Worlds of . . .

### EAGLES
**by Laura Evert**
**Illustrations by John F. McGee**

### FALCONS
**by Wayne Lynch**
**Illustrations by Sherry Neidigh**

### OWLS
**by Wayne Lynch**
**Illustrations by Sherry Neidigh**

### VULTURES
**by Wayne Lynch**
**Illustrations by Sherry Neidigh**

## NorthWord

Minnetonka, Minnesota

Photography © 2005 Wayne Lynch
except: W. Perry Conway: p. 4; Robin Brandt: pp. 16-17; Henry H. Holdsworth/Wild by Nature: pp. 6, 13, 43; Jeff Foott: pp. 7, 45; Michael Quinton/Minden Pictures: p. 8; Lee Kline: pp. 10-11, 39; Michael H. Francis: cover, pp. 14, 18, 34, 36, 44; Tom & Pat Leeson: pp. 20, 25, 30, 31, 46; Greg Baer: pp. 22-23; Dominique Braud/Dembinsky Photo Assoc.: pp. 26-27, 35; Anthony Mercieca/Dembinsky Photo Assoc.: p. 32; Alan G. Nelson/Dembinsky Photo Assoc.: pp. 40-41; Dr. Gordon Court: p. 54, 88-89; Donald M. Jones: p. 72.

Eagles illustrations by John F. McGee. Falcons, Owls, and Vultures illustrations by Sherry Neidigh.

NorthWord
11571 K-Tel Drive
Minnetonka, MN 55343
1-888-255-9989
www.tnkidsbooks.com

**Library of Congress Cataloging-in-Publication Data**
  Birds of prey / by Laura Evert and Wayne Lynch ; illustrations by Sherry Neidigh and John F. McGee.
    p. cm. -- (Our wild world)
  Includes index.
  ISBN 1-55971-925-7 (hardcover)
  1. Birds of prey--Juvenile literature. I. Evert, Laura. II. Lynch, Wayne.
III. Neidigh, Sherry, ill. IV. McGee, John F., ill. V. Title. VI. Our wild world series.

  QL677.78.E94 2005
  598.9–dc22

                                                      2005000189

Printed in Singapore          10  9  8  7  6  5  4  3  2  1

# BIRDS OF PREY

## TABLE OF CONTENTS

*Explore the Fascinating World of . . .*

# Eagles

HAVE YOU EVER wondered how the bald eagle got its name? The answer may not be what you think. The name actually comes from the Old English word "balde," which means "white." And when you look at the white-feathered head of a bald eagle, that certainly makes sense!

Eagles belong to the same family of birds that includes hawks and buzzards. Around the world there are about sixty different species (SPEE-sees), or kinds, of eagles that are divided into four groups. Sea eagles live near water and feed mostly on fish. Snake eagles live near marshes and, as you can guess, eat snakes and other reptiles. Crested eagles have pointed feathers that stand up on top of their head. Booted eagles (also called true eagles) have feathers on their legs that go all the way down to their feet.

Seeing a bald eagle is often a dream come true for many bird watchers.

Bald eagles are good parents that build sturdy nests for their young.

Eagles build their nest up high so they have a clear view
of their territory and hunting area.

Every continent except Antarctica is home to at least one species of eagle. Bald eagles belong to the group of sea eagles. They can be found almost everywhere in North America—from Alaska and Canada to northern Mexico, and in every other U.S. state except Hawaii. The only other eagle that can be found on this continent is the golden eagle, which is a booted eagle.

There are probably more golden eagles than any other kind of eagle in the world today. They can be found as far north as Alaska and Newfoundland, and south along the Rocky Mountains and Pacific Coast to central Mexico. A few golden eagles can be found in the Appalachian Mountains, south to North Carolina. They also live across most of Europe and Asia, south to northern Africa.

A habitat is a specific place in the environment where animals (or people) can live. Golden eagles prefer to live in remote, rugged areas such as mountains, ravines, deserts, and prairies. They make their nests on rocky ledges, in caves found on cliffs, or sometimes in tall trees that stand alone. A bald eagle's habitat is usually a wooded area along a river, stream, or lake shoreline.

Good habitat for bald eagles must include two things: tall trees in which they can build their nests, and fresh water where they can find plenty of fish for food. Although fish is the bald eagle's favorite meal, it also eats rabbits, squirrels, muskrats, birds, small rodents such as mice, and sometimes ducks and other waterfowl. Bald eagles also eat carrion (KARE-ee-un), or dead animals, that they find on the ground or along roadsides.

Pages 8-9: Golden eagles are always on the lookout for food. Their concentration is keen.

Golden eagles are excellent hunters, and do not eat as much carrion as do bald eagles. And although golden eagles do not eat fish, they eat many of the same animals that bald eagles eat, as well as foxes, crows, tortoises, and some snakes. They may even catch and eat skunks and wild goats!

The feathers on any bird are called its plumage (PLOO-mij). An adult bald eagle is easy to recognize with its white head and tail feathers. The rest of its plumage is dark brown. Golden eagles have goldish feathers on the back of their head and neck. The plumage on their body is rich brown.

An eagle has over 7,000 feathers on its head and body. Yet all those feathers combined weigh only about 1 pound (454 grams)!

**Eagles**

# FUNFACT:

The bald eagle's scientific name is *Haliaeetus leucocephalus*.
The golden eagle's scientific name is *Aquila chrysaetos*.

All birds clean their feathers often. It is called preening
and is a very important part of eagle life.

The eagle's body is designed perfectly for a bird that spends much of its time soaring above the trees or just over a lake's surface, looking for its next meal. Many of the bones in the wings and body of an eagle are completely hollow and filled with air. The entire skeleton of an eagle only weighs half as much as its feathers, about 8 ounces (227 grams).

The strong, heavy muscles that power the wings make up almost half of the bird's total weight. Female eagles are larger than male eagles. Adult female eagles weigh up to 14 pounds (6.3 kilograms). Males weigh about 7 to 10 pounds (3.2 to 4.5 kilograms). Eagles that live in northern regions are usually larger than those that live farther south.

The eagle's strong wings make it easy to navigate in the air. A bird may sometimes need to change direction very quickly.

An eagle's long, broad wings have wingtip feathers that can be moved individually, making the eagle extremely agile (AJ-il), or quick and light. These feathers are called primaries. When eagles fly, the primary feathers spread apart and bend up at the tips. By moving the primaries the eagle can easily control its flight direction. The top of the wing is made up of feathers called secondaries.

The eagle's rounded tail is made up of twelve feathers, each of which is 10 to 16 inches (25 to 40 centimeters) long.

Eagles molt, or lose and replace most of their feathers, once every year. All of the feathers are not lost at the same time—it happens gradually. It can sometimes take many months for the shed feathers to be replaced. The feathers on the eagle's head are replaced first.

Eagles can glide over long distances without ever flapping their wings. They use warm currents of air, called updrafts or thermals, to propel themselves upward. Then they either float downward at a long, gentle slope or spiral down in great circles. When they want to soar higher they simply glide into an updraft that lifts them. The wingspan of a female eagle, from tip to tip, can be 8 feet (2.4 meters) long. A male's wingspan is about 6.5 feet (2 meters) long.

When flying through the air eagles can reach speeds of up to 40 miles per hour (64 kilometers per hour). But it is their diving speed that is most useful. Eagles sometimes hunt for prey (PRAY), or the animals on which they feed, while soaring high in the air or perched in a tall tree or on a cliff. When they see something that looks like food they swoop down at speeds of over 100 miles per hour (160 kilometers per hour) and grab the prey with their claws. Then they fly away, carrying their prey to a place where they can eat it.

When prey animals are not plentiful, bald eagles search for carrion.
This helps keep their environment free of some diseases.

An eagle's talons and beak are made of keratin, the same material that makes up human hair and fingernails.

Eagles need good eyesight to help them locate prey. Both the golden's dark eyes and the bald's yellow eyes are extra sharp. The vision of an eagle is believed to be 6 to 8 times better than that of a human. Scientists who study animals are called zoologists (zoe-OL-uh-jists). They believe that an eagle in flight can see a rabbit on the ground from up to 2 miles (3.2 kilometers) away! That's why we use the phrase "eagle-eyed" to describe someone who is good at noticing things that others may miss.

Eagles have binocular (by-NOK-yoo-ler) vision, which means that they can see with both of their eyes at the same time. They also have monocular (muh-NOK-yoo-ler) vision, which means they can also see out of one eye at a time. Having both kinds of vision gives eagles a wide field of view. However, they can only move their eyes a little within the eye sockets, so they must turn their whole head to fully see from side to side.

Eagles also have the ability to see colors better than other birds and animals can. But the trade-off for being able to see in color is that eagles do not see well at night, so they hunt mostly in daylight.

After skimming the surface of a pond and grabbing onto a fish, the eagle holds it tightly until it is ready to eat.

In addition to a regular eyelid, eagles also have a transparent membrane that crosses each eye sideways. As it moves across the eye, the membrane cleans and moistens the eye about once every 5 seconds. It also helps protect the eye from being accidentally pecked by hungry chicks at feeding time.

The eyes are not the only part of a bald eagle that is yellow. Both bald and golden eagles have feet that are covered with bright yellow, scaly skin.

Each foot has four strong toes. Three toes point forward and one points backward. Eagles can tightly curl their toes together and use them to grasp objects like we do with our hands.

Each toe has a black talon, or claw, that is 2 inches (5 centimeters) long. The talons can be used as weapons, but they are mostly used for catching prey. When the eagle swoops down to catch a meal, the razor-sharp talons dig into the prey and hold it securely during the flight back to the nest or other feeding place.

## Eagles
## FUNFACT:

Eagles are found on U.S. coins and paper money. They are also found on postage stamps from around the world, including the U.S. and Canada.

The bald eagle's hooked beak is also bright yellow. A golden eagle's beak is gray with a yellow cere (SEAR). The cere is a waxy knob at the base of the beak where the bird's nostrils are located. An eagle's beak is about 3 inches (7.6 centimeters) long and is sometimes used as a weapon. It is sharp and strong, and is used to tear apart prey before the eagle eats it. Eagles do not chew their food. Instead, they rip it into chunks and swallow the pieces whole.

Bald eagles prefer to eat fish, especially the kinds that feed near the surface of the water, because they are easier to catch. They do not plunge or dive into the water to catch fish as do some other birds. Instead, they skim across the surface of the water, and when they see a fish that looks easy to catch they swing their legs down into the water and grab the fish with their powerful talons.

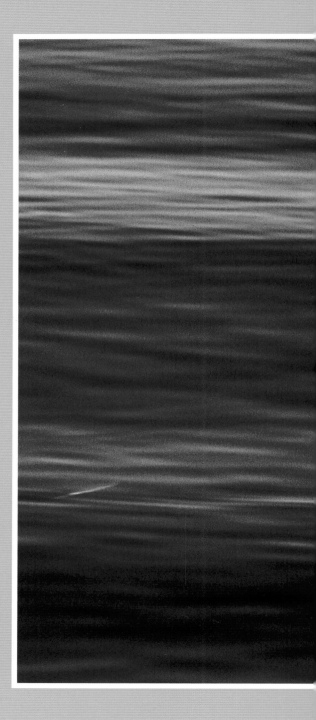

Eagles swing their feet forcefully down into the water
so their talons can grab fish.

The bald eagle also has another way to get fish for dinner, but this method is more sly. When it sees another bird, such as an osprey (AH-spray), catch a fish, the eagle flies at the unsuspecting bird in a rush. The other bird, which is usually smaller and not as fierce, often drops the fish while trying to escape the eagle. The eagle then grabs the fish in midair and flies away to enjoy its stolen meal.

A high place such as a cliff ledge or a branch in a tree is the perfect place for an eagle to eat. High above the ground the eagle can keep a sharp lookout for predators (PRED-uh-tors), or enemies, while enjoying its meal. After the food is quickly torn into pieces and swallowed, it is stored in a pouch in the eagle's throat called the crop. The crop allows the bird to eat large amounts of food when there is plenty and store some for later, when hunting may be more difficult. The crop can hold as much as 1.5 pounds (680 grams) of meat.

When there are chicks to feed, the eagle still finds a perch where it can eat some of the food itself before giving the rest away to the hungry little mouths back at the nest.

A fresh salmon taken from the icy waters of a river makes a good meal for this eagle in winter.

Chicks must be fed several times a day,
which means many hunting trips for the parent.

Eagle nests are huge! Bald eagles usually select a tall, strong tree surrounded by some open space for a nest site. This makes it easier for the birds to come and go. Or the nest might be built in the crotch of a tree, usually just below the top. This gives the bird places to perch, and provides a good base on which to build the nest.

Many eagles build both a main nest and a second nest, often just a short distance away. Zoologists are not sure why they do this. It may be to confuse predators such as owls and raccoons that are a threat to the eggs and chicks. Or, the second nest may be built as a back-up to the main nest, in case the first nest is destroyed just before egg-laying. And if the adults are unable to produce eggs or chicks one year, they may try using the other nest the next year.

A bald eagle's nest is called an aerie (AIR-ee). The birds build and add to their nests by stacking sticks together. They carefully weave the sticks as though they were making a basket. The female does most of the work. A new nest that is 4 feet (1.2 meters) high and 5 feet (1.5 meters) across can be built in just a few days.

## Eagles
# FUNFACT:

The largest bald eagle nest on record measured almost 10 feet (3 meters) across and over 20 feet (6 meters) deep, and weighed over 4,000 pounds (1,800 kilograms).

The nest is usually lined with soft grasses and leaves to cushion the eggs. The nest's high edge prevents the chicks from tumbling out. More nesting material is added throughout the season to cover waste in the nest. Eagles are "messy" birds. They eat in the nest and do not throw out the left-overs!

This pine makes a good tree for an eagle nest. It is tall and the limbs are strong.

Every year eagles repair damage to their nest and add more twigs and sticks. If a pair of eagles uses the same nest year after year, the nest may reach a height and weight so great that it topples the tree. An old nest that is reused many times may be over 8 feet (2.4 meters) across and weigh up to 2,000 pounds (907 kilograms)—about the same size as a small truck! Some eagle nests have lasted a hundred years.

After the adults make the nest improvements for the season, the female lays the eggs. Exactly when an eagle lays its eggs depends on where it lives. In southern regions like Florida, eagles may begin laying eggs as early as November, while eagles farther north do not usually lay eggs until April. Birds in the North wait until the frozen waterways begin to thaw because they must be able to find fish.

Eagles sometimes build their nests on cliffs, like this one in Alaska.

Bald eagle eggs are incubated for about 35 days before the chicks are ready to hatch.
Golden eagle eggs like these can take up to 45 days to hatch.

Bald eagles usually lay one or two eggs, ocassionally even three eggs. Golden eagles lay up to four eggs, but two eggs is most common. A day or two passes between the laying of each egg. The eggs of the bald eagle are white. Golden eagle eggs are white too, but sometimes they have brown blotches on them.

After the eggs are laid, one adult sits on them almost all the time, especially during stormy or cold weather. The female spends the most time incubating the eggs, but the male takes a turn when she leaves the nest to hunt for food. Sometimes the male brings food to his mate while she sits on the eggs.

The eggs are gently turned every so often to provide even warmth. This prevents the embryo (EM-bree-oh), or developing chick, from sticking to the inside of the shell.

Before the chicks hatch, the adults can hear them calling out from inside their shell. Sometimes it takes a chick nearly a whole day to break out of its shell. It uses a little tooth on the end of the beak called an egg tooth, which soon falls off.

Since the eggs were laid at different times, they hatch a few days apart. The first hatchling out of its shell has the advantage and often wins the fight for food. Without enough to eat, the second chick sometimes does not survive. Stormy weather and disease are also dangers for chicks, and some years only 50 percent of all eagle chicks survive.

Eagle chicks are called eaglets. They have coats of soft, gray down. The eaglets are only about 4 inches (10 centimeters) long and may weigh just 2 ounces (60 grams).

## Eagles
# FUNFACT:

Eagles often nest within 100 miles (160 kilometers) of the place they were born. They usually mate for life, and can live to be over 30 years old.

Eaglets cry out for food almost as soon as they hatch.

For the first two weeks one adult is always at the nest to protect the chicks from harm and the cold. The male eagle usually brings them food. Sometimes the female does not allow him to eat at the nest with the rest of the family. The female gently places bits of food into the chick's mouth. As the eaglets grow, the parents provide protection and food—and shade on hot days.

By the end of four weeks the eaglets begin growing a darker down coat in place of the gray one. They are clumsy, but soon learn to stand. During this time both of the parents share hunting and feeding duties. Every three hours fresh food is brought to the nest to feed the ravenous, or very hungry, chicks.

This young, or immature, bald eagle stretches its wings to become stronger as it learns to fly from the nest.

This young bald eagle has found a good perch. It is learning to watch for prey on the ground below so it can hunt for itself.

Until now, the eaglets patiently waited while the adults tore up their food into small bits. After about eight weeks, the food is torn into larger pieces and the young eagles boldly snatch the food that is tossed in front of them.

At nine weeks old, the chicks are nearly full grown. They are active and noisy and constantly demand food. The eaglets also spend a lot of time jumping and flapping in the nest as they get ready to learn to fly. Finally, when they are ten to twelve weeks old they are ready to fledge, or leave the nest and fly for the first time. Their coats of down have been replaced by dark brown feathers.

Young golden eagles have a white tail with a dark brown band on the bottom edge and some white on their wings. Bald eagles do not have white feathers on their head or tail until they are about four or five years old. And that is when both kinds of eagles are ready to mate for the first time.

## Eagles
# FUNFACT:

Don't let the light weight of an eagle feather fool you. Pound for pound an eagle wing is as strong as the wing of an airplane!

Some eagles glide gracefully out of the nest on their first attempt to fly, but then struggle as they try to land on a perch. If an eaglet crashes to the ground during its early attempts at flight, the parents stay nearby. They call out to the young one, providing protection and encouragement until the excited young bird tries to fly again.

While learning to fly, young eagles still rely on their parents for food. Feeding may take place at a perch away from the nest. When they are twenty weeks old the young are nearly able to take care of themselves. In northern regions, it is almost time for migration out of the nesting territory to warmer areas. Some southern eagles move north to avoid the heat. Young eagles migrating for the first time usually have to travel farther to find a territory that is not already occupied by other eagles.

Young eagles stay with their parents even after they have grown
to their full size. They separate when they migrate.

It is more common to see a golden eagle near the ground,
because it hunts more land prey than the bald eagle.

Many golden eagles do not migrate at all if there is plenty of food in their territory. Adult bald eagles may only migrate as far as necessary to find an area with plenty of food. Golden eagles sometimes have a hunting territory of over 160 square miles (414 square kilometers). An adult bald eagle's territory is usually smaller than 10 square miles (26 square kilometers).

Most eagles, especially goldens, prefer to live away from other eagles, except for their mates. But in areas where there is plenty of food to go around it is not unusual to see many bald eagles living peacefully together. These eagles may even share food. In some parts of Alaska, up to 4,000 bald eagles may gather to feast on migrating salmon.

## Eagles
# FUNFACT:

The golden eagle is the national bird of Mexico. And even though Benjamin Franklin suggested the turkey, Congress made the bald eagle the national symbol of the United States in 1782.

When they must, eagles defend their territory in several ways. Sometimes they soar high in the air, circling their land for other birds to see. Other times they perch in the branches of the highest tree, keeping watch for intruders. When one eagle crosses into another's territory, the resident quickly charges and chases the intruder away. If a mated pair has claimed the territory, both the male and female defend it. It is common to see one eagle perched in a tree on one side of a lake and its mate perched in a tree on the opposite side.

As they watch for trespassers, the pair calls back and forth to each other. Bald eagles have a high-pitched, thin voice that seems weak for such a big bird. Their call sounds like a string of cackles, first going up and then down in pitch. Some people think it sounds like a giggle. Golden eagles are usually silent. When they do call, it sounds like a scream or high-pitched *"kee-kee-kee"* squeal.

## Eagles
# FUNFACT:

Sometimes the fish that an eagle grabs is so heavy that the eagle cannot immediately fly into the air. To build up speed before it takes off, the eagle can "row" across the water, using its wings as oars.

These parents are flying back to the nest with a
freshly caught fish to feed the hungry eaglets.

Native Americans have great respect for both bald eagles and golden eagles. Some tribes considered the bald eagle to be equal to humans. Other tribes used eagle feathers in ceremonial costumes and celebrations, while still other tribes decorated only the bravest warriors with eagle feathers.

Eagles may live year-round in cold-weather climates as long as there is enough food.

At one time there were probably up to 500,000 bald eagles in North America. By 1963 there were less than 500 pairs of eagles in the lower U.S. Their survival was threatened in several ways, including hunting and loss of habitat. Big birds need big areas of land on which to find food and raise their young. As more and more people populated the continent, life became difficult for eagles. In 1967 the bald eagle was an endangered species.

The most severe threat to bald eagles was the use of a pesticide called DDT. People used it to kill mosquitoes and other insects. Since bald eagles mainly ate fish that ate the poisoned insects, the birds consumed large amounts of the poison. DDT would stay in the body of an eagle for many years. It caused the eggs to have thin, weak shells that would break as they were laid or when the female tried to incubate them. Because of this, very few new chicks were hatched for many years.

Eagles gather in the same area if prey is plentiful.

In the air or on the ground, the white head of an adult bald eagle makes it easy to identify.

In 1972 people were no longer allowed to use DDT, and gradually eagles were able to recover. Finally, in 1995, the bald eagle population in all of the lower 48 states had increased enough for them to be listed as threatened instead of endangered. Fortunately, the golden eagle did not suffer as much DDT poisoning since its prey is mostly grass-eating animals.

Today there are about 5,800 pairs of bald eagles in the lower U.S. and over 100,000 bald eagles in Alaska and Canada. Environmental groups are working together to set aside protected land for bald and golden eagles to use as their territories. Zoologists are finding ways to improve the survival rate of eaglets. And people are constructing platforms on which eagles can build their nests and raise their young.

With so many people working hard for eagle survival, we can hope that future generations will always be able to watch eagles soar and glide across the open sky.

## Eagles
# FUNFACT:

**If you want to see large numbers of bald eagles, a good place to go is near Haines, Alaska. Or you can attend a bald eagle festival in cities like Rock Island, Illinois; Dubuque, Iowa; or Emery, Texas.**

# My BIRDS OF PREY Adventures

The date of my adventure: _____

The people who came with me: _____

_____

Where I went: _____

What birds of prey I saw:

_____    _____

_____    _____

_____    _____

_____    _____

The date of my adventure: _____

The people who came with me: _____

_____

Where I went: _____

What birds of prey I saw:

_____    _____

_____    _____

_____    _____

_____    _____

# My BIRDS OF PREY Adventures

The date of my adventure: _____

The people who came with me: _____

_____

Where I went: _____

What birds of prey I saw:

_____          _____

_____          _____

_____          _____

_____          _____

The date of my adventure: _____

The people who came with me: _____

_____

Where I went: _____

What birds of prey I saw:

_____          _____

_____          _____

_____          _____

_____          _____

**49**

*Explore the Fascinating World of* . . .

# Falcons

IN ALL THE WORLD, there are 61 kinds, or species (SPEE-sees), of falcons. Only five of them breed in the United States and Canada, but they include two of the most famous of these birds. One is the Arctic-nesting gyrfalcon (JEER-fal-con), the largest, most powerful falcon in the world. The other is the crow-size peregrine (PER-uh-gren) falcon, possibly the fastest-flying bird on Earth. The peregrine is also one of the most widespread birds in the world and lives on every continent except Antarctica.

The other three falcons include the merlin, which nests in the northern prairies and forests of Canada and Alaska. The second is the prairie falcon, which lives on the hot, dry western prairies and deserts. The third is the American kestrel (KESS-trel).

The kestrel is the smallest falcon in Canada and the United States. It is only slightly larger than a robin. The kestrel hunts in open areas throughout the two countries as well as in city parks and fields, cemeteries, airports, and golf courses.

Peregrine falcon chicks less than one year old have dark streaks on their feathers. Some of the streaks fade as they get older.

Gyrfalcons often hunt along the edge of the ocean in Canada, as far as 800 miles (1,288 kilometers) north of the Arctic Circle.

Adult American kestrels catch and kill deer mice for a meal.
They may hunt in the grassy ditch beside a highway.

Falcons, like hawks and eagles, are birds of prey (PRAY), or raptors (RAP-ters). They hunt and eat other animals. All five of the falcons in the United States and Canada hunt birds. Some of them specialize more than others.

The gyrfalcon of the Arctic, for example, mainly hunts birds such as willow ptarmigan (TAR-mih-gun) and rock ptarmigan. A family of gyrfalcons may eat 200 ptarmigan during the four months of their summer nesting season. This is the time that young falcons are in the nest and must be fed by their parents.

The merlin, on the other hand, is a fierce hunter of small to medium songbirds such as robins, starlings, swallows, and sparrows. Out West, the prairie falcon hunts horned larks, meadow larks, and mourning doves.

Because the kestrel is so small, it hunts grasshoppers, dragonflies, scorpions, spiders, and lizards more often than it hunts birds. Scientists in New York State, however, watched one kestrel hunting at a colony of nesting bank swallows. It caught chicks as they crowded at the opening of the family nest burrows.

The hungriest swallow chicks would sit as close as possible to the mouth of the burrow so they could get as much food as possible when their parents came to feed them. The kestrel hung upside down above the burrows by one foot and grabbed the chubby chicks with its other foot. In one day, the falcon caught nine swallow chicks in a row while hunting like this. For some of the chicks, it was not a good idea to be so greedy!

The most famous bird hunter among the five falcons is the peregrine. Although this bold raptor commonly hunts shorebirds and ducks, nothing with feathers is safe from attack. Scientists who study birds are called ornithologists (or-nih-THOL-uh-jists). They have made a list of the birds that peregrines eat. In North America, the list includes over 425 species, more than half of the birds that live there. Worldwide, the peregrine hunts more than 2,000 different birds!

The list is even longer if you include those birds that the peregrine doesn't plan to eat and just wants to scare away from its nest and young. If a peregrine parent thinks its chicks are in danger, it will bravely attack birds much bigger than itself, including hawks, owls, ravens, vultures, cranes, and geese. One bold peregrine even attacked a bald eagle, killing it with a blow to its head.

## Falcons
# FUNFACT:

Hunting falcons commonly miss more prey than they catch. When peregrines hunt fast-flying shorebirds they may only succeed at 1 in 10 attempts. They do better when they are hunting insects and small mammals, which do not see as well as birds.

In the autumn, young and inexperienced ducks are easy prey for peregrine falcons.

Even though the falcons of Canada and the United States prefer birds, they also eat many other creatures. For example, in some areas of the Arctic, gyrfalcons hunt Arctic hares, and peregrines hunt lemmings. On the west coast of Canada, hungry peregrines will even eat green, slimy banana slugs, and kestrels will consume earthworms. Along the Snake River in Idaho, prairie falcons catch so many Townsend's ground squirrels that many prairie falcons are able to nest close together in record numbers.

Falcons are also not afraid of bats. They eat any they can catch, as well as mice, voles, or shrews that scamper into view.

The bare skin at the base of a falcon's beak is called the cere (SER). The yellow cere on this kestrel indicates that the bird is healthy.

Sometimes falcons catch more food than they can eat. When they do, they store the extra meals in a hiding place. This storing behavior is called caching (CASH-ing). Some favorite places for falcons to cache are in crevices on high cliffs, under a bush, in a large clump of grass, in an old raven or hawk nest, or in a hollow tree.

Falcons usually cache extra food any time they can, but they do it most often in the winter and during the summer nesting season when they are busy raising chicks. In winter, high winds and snowstorms make hunting difficult and falcons may not hunt or eat for several days. This is when the food they stored earlier may save their lives.

During the nesting season, parent falcons must catch much more prey than usual because they must feed their hungry chicks many times every day. If the parents have a bad day of hunting they can give the extra food they cached to their chicks. One peregrine that nested in Boise, Idaho, cached more than 20 mourning doves on a building's window ledge near its nest.

## Falcons
## FUNFACT:

**Most falcons have a dark streak on their face below their eyes. This may reduce glare and help the birds see better in bright sunshine. Football players smear black shoe polish under their eyes for the same reason.**

Falconers cover the eyes of their birds with a special leather hood when they take them to a new location. This keeps the birds quiet and relaxed.

Perhaps as long ago as 4,000 years, humans began to trap, tame, and train peregrines and other falcons to hunt for them. This was the beginning of the sport we now call falconry. In ancient times, falconry was the sport of kings and emperors. One powerful emperor in ancient China owned 200 gyrfalcons, as well as 300 other falcons and hawks. He had 10,000 workers whose only job was to find prey for his falcons on hunting expeditions.

In those days, falcons were extremely valuable, sometimes worth more than gold. Royalty and other powerful people often used falcons as expensive gifts and rewards. Sometimes falcons were used as payment for ransoms. One captured prince in medieval Europe was freed from prison only after his family delivered a dozen priceless white gyrfalcons from distant Greenland.

Even today, the gift of a rare falcon may impress a king. The royal family of Saudi Arabia has a great love of falconry. In the 1980s, the Prime Minister of Canada gave a white gyrfalcon to the King of Saudi Arabia as a gift of friendship.

Gyrfalcons vary in color from all white with some scattered dark markings on their back to dark gray all over. White birds are most common in the Arctic.

Hungry juvenile merlins scream loudly at a parent as it approaches with fresh food in its talons.

Worldwide, the sport of falconry has probably never been more popular than it is today. In the United States and Canada, there are approximately 3,600 falconers. Today most falconers use their birds for sport hunting, but some use them for business. Airports in many large cities, including Chicago, New York, Milwaukee, Montreal, and Vancouver, hire falconers to fly their trained birds over the runways. The falcons scare away gulls, ducks, and geese that can fly into the planes and cause serious accidents or damage.

Falcons hunt in several different ways. The most common way is to sit and wait quietly on an elevated place such as the top of a telephone pole, tree, or cliff. At other times they soar high over their hunting area to search for prey.

All falcons are strong flyers and sometimes they hunt by flying close to the ground using low hills, rocky ridges, and bushes to hide their approach. They hunt like this to surprise birds and animals and scare them into the open where they can be attacked more easily.

Another way for some falcons to hunt is to hover (HUH-ver), but hovering is hard work. The large peregrine is too heavy to hunt this way, but the small kestrel can hover better than any other raptor.

When a flying kestrel locates a meal it may immediately begin to hover, no higher than the roof on a house. A kestrel can hover for as long as a minute, and even longer if there is a strong wind. When the moment is right, the bird drops like a rock and grabs its prey.

An adult peregrine falcon has a wingspan of about 40 inches (1 meter). Male and female peregrines look similar except that the female is larger and heavier.

For many falcon lovers the power dive is the most exciting type of hunting to watch, and peregrines do it best. To see how fast a peregrine could dive, a skydiver who was also a falconer jumped out of a plane with his trained peregrine at 12,000 feet (3,658 meters). That's over 2 miles (3.5 kilometers) high in the sky. As the skydiver did a free fall, the peregrine flew along with him and the man was able to estimate the falcon's speed. With its wings pulled tight against its body, the falcon flew at 200 miles (322 kilometers) per hour. It looked like a feathered rocket! The skydiver was unable to see if the peregrine could fly faster because he had to stop the experiment and open his parachute.

## Falcons
# FUNFACT:

**Many peregrines migrate as far south as Central and South America. They make round trips of over 10,000 miles (16,000 kilometers).**

The feet of a one-month-old prairie falcon are almost as large as its parents' feet. But the young bird is still not strong enough to kill for itself.

When a falcon catches its prey, the prey is usually still alive. Like most birds of prey, a falcon has feet that are tough and strong. On the end of each toe is a long, sharp claw, called a talon. Falcons do not kill prey with their feet, but with their sharp beak. They bite the prey on the head or on the back of the neck while holding it in their talons. Hawks and eagles use their long talons and powerful grip to squeeze their prey over and over again until it dies.

All falcons have a special tooth, called a tomial (TOE-mee-ul) tooth, on the sharp edge of the upper beak. Ornithologists believe that falcons use this tooth to cut or injure the spinal cord of their prey when they bite it on the neck. The tomial tooth may help falcons kill prey that is larger than themselves.

Falcons need clean, healthy feathers to hunt and fly fast, and to stay warm in winter and dry in summer. They may spend several hours every day caring for their feathers.

All falcons bathe when they can. A peregrine will step into the water up to its belly at the edge of a stream and dip its head underwater over and over again. At the same time, it raises its feathers, flutters its wings and tail, and lets the water wash over its back. Merlins and gyrfalcons do the same.

## Falcons
## FUNFACT:

The prairie falcon is usually found far away from water sources. The peregrine falcon is almost always found near a river or lake.

When everything freezes in winter, a gyrfalcon may bathe in soft, fluffy snow to clean its feathers. In the desert where water is scarce, the prairie falcon bathes on the bare ground and dusts its feathers with powdery dirt. Scientists think the dry dirt works like mosquito repellent to keep lice and ticks away. Other falcon species also take dust baths. Researchers watched a merlin that had many lice on its body dust itself seven times in one hour. The lice and ticks feed on the falcon's blood and make the bird itch.

## Falcons
## FUNFACT:

In captivity, kestrels and merlins may live for 10 years. Prairie falcons, peregrines, and gyrfalcons may live for 20 years or more. In the wild life is much harder and most wild falcons live only half as long as they do in captivity.

The merlin can survive the cold of a northern winter as long as it can find enough food to eat and keep its body warm.

When a peregrine falcon captures prey, it may spread its wings and huddle over the animal. This helps hide it and guard it from other falcons.

Besides dusting their feathers and washing them with water or snow, falcons also wipe a special oil on their feathers. This is called preening. The oil comes from the preen gland, on the bird's rump at the base of its tail.

The falcon gently squeezes the gland with its beak and rubs its head over it. Then it uses its beak and its head to spread the oil to the other feathers on its body. The oil keeps the feathers from drying and cracking, and also protects them from harmful bacteria and fungi that may damage them.

Sleek, shiny feathers are a good clue that a falcon is well fed and healthy. Female falcons need a strong, healthy partner to help them raise their chicks. So, at the start of every breeding season, the females observe males to see which ones would make good partners, or mates.

Some falcons stay with the same partner for many years, and some choose a new partner every year. If a falcon's partner dies or disappears, the remaining bird usually finds another mate quickly.

Peregrines begin to preen when they are just eight days old. As adults they may spend
several hours each day caring for their feathers in this way.

American kestrels can hover in one spot for almost one minute. When the wind is blowing strongly they can do it even longer, but it takes lots of energy.

To be a good partner, a male falcon needs more than sleek, shiny feathers. He must also be a strong flyer and a good hunter.

For these reasons, when a male falcon is courting a female he tries to impress her with his flying and hunting skills. He circles and soars high above her, screaming loudly. He performs steep power dives and climbs, and flies past the female as fast as he can, doing difficult half-rolls, dips, and swerves to show off.

This kind of flying takes a lot of strength and energy and if the male is not healthy the female will probably notice.

Sometimes the female joins the male and soars and screams with him. He may climb above her and dive at her over and over again, or chase close behind her in a high-speed race. One peregrine may fly upside down beneath the other and the pair may grab each other's talons briefly. The birds may even touch each other's beak in midair.

## Falcons
# FUNFACT:

Falcons are quiet most of the year. They use their loud voices mainly during the spring and summer when they are courting, and to frighten away enemies.

A peregrine nest is nothing more than a depression in the sand created by the mother's body. The parents add no sticks, grass, feathers, or greenery to their nest.

When the courting falcons finally land they usually perch, or sit, close together. They may stay like this for hours. Sometimes they preen each other's head feathers, or gently nibble on each other's beak and toes. Once the female chooses a male to be her partner, she sits and waits, while he hunts, and hunts, and hunts.

The male does all the hunting for both of them for at least two months. He may hunt for one whole month before the female lays her first egg, and then continue for another month while she incubates (INK-you-bates) the eggs. After that, he feeds the newly hatched chicks as well as their mother, who needs to stay with the babies to keep them warm.

By the time the baby falcons are about two weeks old their fluffy, down feathers are thick enough to keep them warm. Then the mother can leave and go hunting for herself.

A female falcon sometimes turns upside down to catch the prey dropped by her mate. They both continue flying!

When the male makes a food delivery to his mate it can be spectacular to watch. He may fly past her carrying prey and screaming loudly. If she stays perched where she is, she may scream back at him to bring the food.

Female falcons are always larger and more powerful than their mates, so a male falcon delivering food may be afraid to land near a hungry female, even if she is his partner. Instead, he may drop the food in midair for her to catch. Or he may pass it to her, foot-to-foot, as she swoops upside down beneath him.

The female falcon's feet are dangerous weapons and the male must be careful not to be injured accidentally.

A pair of falcons will breed in an area only if there is a good place to nest. Even when the hunting is good, the birds will move somewhere else if they cannot find a safe nesting site.

Falcons never build their own nest. For example, merlins often use the old stick nest of a raven, crow, or magpie. Peregrines, gyrfalcons, and prairie falcons may also use the old nests of other birds, but more often they nest on a bare ledge, high on a cliff.

The small kestrel is the least able to defend itself and its young from enemies. For this reason, the kestrel usually hides its nest safely inside an old woodpecker hole, or in a crack in a cliff or hollow tree. Kestrels may even nest inside a box built for them by humans. A group of researchers in Idaho found that kestrels also nested in the wall cracks of abandoned farm buildings, in old chimneys, in hollowed-out fence posts, and even inside drainpipes.

**Falcons**
# FUNFACT:

Kestrels have two dark spots on the back of their neck
that look like large eyes. Ornithologists think the eye spots fool
predators into thinking that the falcon is watching them.
This may discourage them from attacking.

When the American kestrel is perched, it often has the habit of bobbing its head. This movement makes its false eye spots even more convincing to a nearby predator.

After many years, a gyrfalcon nesting ledge gets stained with droppings. Orange jewel lichens (LIKE-enz) grow well in these droppings and biologists can often find hidden nests by looking for these patches of orange on the cliffs.

Falcons prefer cliff ledges that have a floor of loose dirt or fine gravel, and an overhang that protects them from hail and rain and shades them from the hot afternoon sun. In some areas, such ledges are rare, so when the falcons find one, they may use it for a long time.

Researchers in Alaska found a ledge that had been used by nesting peregrines for at least 100 years. A gyrfalcon nesting ledge discovered in Arctic Canada was used for so many years that it was buried under 2 feet (60 centimeters) of bones mixed with old falcon droppings. The bones belonged to Arctic hares eaten by the birds.

Ornithologists in England have discovered a ledge that peregrines have used for over 800 years. In Australia, falcons have used one ledge for at least 16,000 years! At the beginning of that time, there were no humans living in North America, and most of Canada was buried under ice 1 mile (1.6 kilometers) thick. In California, there were elephants and sabertooth tigers roaming the land.

Most birds of prey tend to avoid humans and nest away from cities and their skyscrapers. However, in the last 25 years, two species of falcons have settled into city life.

Some merlins that used to nest in the prairies of Canada and fly south every winter now live year-round in large prairie cities such as Calgary, Edmonton, Saskatoon, and Regina. These adaptable falcons live in the suburbs and nest in evergreen trees where there are old nests built by crows and magpies, and where there is a steady supply of house sparrows for food. One ornithologist called house sparrows "rats with wings" because there are so many of them living in our cities. It seems the merlins have discovered this and are taking advantage of it.

## Falcons
# FUNFACT:

Some falcons have been given nicknames. The American kestrel is called the sparrow hawk. Peregrine falcons are known as duck hawks. Merlins are pigeon hawks.

For six years, this female peregrine falcon nested on the same ledge on the 15th floor of an office building in Calgary, a city of nearly one million people.

Another urban dweller is the majestic peregrine, which now lives in many cities, including some of the largest, such as New York, Chicago, Milwaukee, and Seattle. Most of these big-city falcons nest on the ledges of high-rise buildings surrounded by traffic and crowds. They hunt pigeons, robins, and starlings, swerving and swooping between towers of glass and steel.

In some cities, these nesting falcons are observed by hidden video cameras wired to television monitors below. Without disturbing the birds, interested people can watch the peregrines as they raise their chicks.

All of the falcons in Canada and the United States lay three to five rusty, speckled eggs. Many people think that the reddish eggs of the peregrine are the most beautiful of any bird of prey.

Falcons never line their nests with twigs, leaves, or grass. If the nest is on a bare ledge, the birds simply scrape a shallow hollow in the dirt with their feet to cradle their eggs.

The falcons incubate their eggs for 28 to 35 days. The two largest falcons, the peregrine and the gyrfalcon, incubate the longest.

Female falcons do most of the incubating, although the males may help for one or two hours each day while their partners eat, stretch, and preen. Most male and female falcons have at least two small areas of bare skin on their bellies. These thick, soft patches of featherless skin are called brood patches. They keep the eggs warm. Soon after the eggs hatch, the feathers grow back and cover the skin.

Falcon chicks hatch within one or two days and grow at about the same speed so all the chicks are about the same size.

Both parents are not often at the nest together.
The male must be away hunting much of the time.

Many animals hunt falcon chicks. They are called predators (PRED-uh-torz). Great horned owls, golden eagles, goshawks, Cooper's hawks, red-tailed hawks, ravens, and crows all eat baby falcons.

In Florida, yellow rat snakes and corn snakes may climb into kestrel nests and eat the eggs and young. In Texas, researchers have even watched an army of fire ants swarm into a kestrel's nest and sting the young to death.

Foxes, coyotes, wolves, black bears, grizzlies, and wolverines also consume falcon eggs and chicks.

It is no surprise, then, that adult falcons defend their nest and young with courage and force. An angry peregrine parent will attack any predator that comes near, including a human. Many scientists have been struck and injured by a falcon when they went too close to the bird's nest.

Because peregrines defend their nests so fiercely, other birds sometimes nest close to them to get protection from predators. Researchers have found common eider ducks nesting just 36 yards (33 meters) from a peregrine nest, and Canada geese nesting as close as 8 feet (2.5 meters)!

Many ornithologists believe that the bony flaps inside the nostrils of the peregrine falcon help the bird to breathe easier when it is diving at very high speeds.

When young prairie falcons are about one month old, feathers begin to grow on their wings.

The larger the falcon species, the longer they need to mature. For example, merlin and kestrel chicks leave the nest when they are about four weeks of age. Young prairie falcons and peregrines leave when they are five to six weeks old, and young gyrfalcons leave at seven to eight weeks.

Birds that have left the nest are called fledglings (FLEJ-lings). At first, the fledglings stay close to the nest and close to each other. After a month or so they become brave enough to explore by themselves. They may fly as far away as one-half mile (6.8 kilometers).

Even after the chicks leave the nest, their parents continue to feed them for one or two months. It takes time and practice for fledglings to become skilled hunters. The meals from their parents help them while they are learning.

## Falcons
# FUNFACT:

**Arctic gyrfalcons nest very far north. Their nests have been found on the northern tip of Greenland, only 600 miles (965 kilometers) from the North Pole.**

Play is an important way for young falcons to practice hunting and flying. They chase each other. They dive on birds much larger than themselves, such as geese and ravens, pretending to attack them. They also chase clumps of thistle down blowing in the wind and feathers floating by.

One researcher watched a young peregrine chase a butterfly, and another watched a fledgling prairie falcon play with a dried piece of cow dung. The bird carried the dung into the air, dropped it, then swooped down and caught it again before it hit the ground. The young prairie falcon eventually landed, tossed the dung around, and jumped on it as if it were a mouse.

Some adult peregrine falcons are white. They are from the northwestern coast of Hudson Bay in Canada.

Most young merlins migrate south from Alaska and Canada in August. They spend the winter in Mexico, Central America, or South America.

By the time most fledgling falcons are three months old they have left the nest and their parents. This is the beginning of the hardest year of their life.

Only one young falcon in four survives to be one year old. Many die from starvation, unable to hunt well enough to feed themselves. Others are killed by owls, hawks, eagles, or other falcons. Some die in crashes with automobiles, power lines, and fences.

Today, the falcons of the United States and Canada are doing quite well. It was a different story about 40 years ago. After World War II, farmers began to spray a chemical called DDT on their crops to kill insect pests.

No one knew at the time that DDT not only killed insects but also made birds sick if they ate the insects. Then, if falcons ate the sick birds, the chemicals also poisoned the falcons. Poisoned falcons could not lay normal eggs. The shells on their eggs were thin and would crack when the parents tried to incubate them. Falcons could no longer raise chicks and the birds started to disappear.

This poison affected peregrines and merlins the most, but the other falcons also suffered. In 1972, the use of DDT was banned in North America. A few years after that, peregrine and merlin numbers slowly began to increase again. Today, these magnificent birds of prey are almost as plentiful as they were earlier.

People learned a valuable lesson from the results of using DDT. It was a warning. If chemicals can poison falcons, they can poison humans as well. If we help care for the environment and keep it clean and free of chemicals, then we and the falcons may continue to live healthy lives.

A prairie falcon will sometimes follow a northern harrier hawk and steal its kill. Or it may capture escaping birds that are frightened by the hawk.

# My BIRDS OF PREY Adventures

The date of my adventure: _____

The people who came with me: _____

_____

Where I went: _____

What birds of prey I saw:

_____     _____

_____     _____

_____     _____

_____     _____

The date of my adventure: _____

The people who came with me: _____

_____

Where I went: _____

What birds of prey I saw:

_____     _____

_____     _____

_____     _____

_____     _____

# My BIRDS OF PREY Adventures

The date of my adventure: _____

The people who came with me: _____

_____

Where I went: _____

What birds of prey I saw:

_____          _____

_____          _____

_____          _____

_____          _____

The date of my adventure: _____

The people who came with me: _____

_____

Where I went: _____

What birds of prey I saw:

_____          _____

_____          _____

_____          _____

_____          _____

# Explore the Fascinating World of . . .
# Owls

WORLDWIDE, THERE ARE OVER 200 kinds, or species (SPEE-sees), of owls. Most live in the dense forests of the hot tropics, and only 19 are found in the United States and Canada. Among these owls is the smallest owl in the world, the elf owl. Another one, the snowy owl, is one of the heaviest and most powerful owls in the world.

The elf owl is no larger than a house sparrow and it would take 60 elf owls to weigh as much as the snowy owl of the Arctic. Just one feather from the end of a snowy's wing is twice as tall as a tiny elf owl. In fact, a hungry snowy owl could gulp down a dozen elf owls for lunch and still be hungry for more.

Owls are found in every corner of the United States and Canada. They live in the deserts of the Southwest, the grasslands of the prairies, and on the Arctic tundra of Alaska. They also live in the Rocky Mountains, in the dark spruce forests of Canada, in the cypress swamps of Florida and Louisiana, and in the forests of New England.

If you love owls, the best places to live are in Washington and British Columbia—each is home to 14 different owl species.

An adult female snowy owl may weigh more than 5 pounds (2.25 kilograms).

The feather ear tufts on a great horned owl have nothing to do with hearing. The bird uses them for display.

In the past, owls were a frequent part of human customs and beliefs. Cherokee Indians believed if you washed a newborn baby's eyes with water in which an owl's feather had been soaked, the child would see better at night. In Europe, people nailed a dead owl over their front door to protect the family from disease. They sometimes killed a second owl and hung its body on their barn to guard against heavy rain, hail, and lightning storms. For many in Europe, an owl was a feathered witch that could forecast the weather, warn of death, or kidnap naughty children.

Today, many people believe it is bad luck to have an owl fly over them. The funniest story about owls claims that if you walk around an owl many times in one direction the bird will twist off its own head! Of course, all of these stories and beliefs are untrue, and the real story about owls is better than any fairy tale.

**Owls**
# FUNFACT:

**A group of owls is called
a parliament (PAR-luh-ment).**

During the day, the western screech owl hides from predators in the thick branches of a tree or bush.

The thick, strong talons on a great horned owl may be almost 1 inch (2.5 centimeters) long.

Owls, like hawks and eagles, are birds of prey (PRAY), or raptors (RAP-torz). They attack, kill, and eat other animals for their food. To do this they need weapons, and an owl's beak and feet are deadly weapons. The beak on all owls is hooked and has razor-sharp edges designed for killing and cutting. Each of the bird's feet has 4 needle-sharp claws, called talons. The feet of many northern owls, such as the great horned, great gray, boreal, and snowy owl, are covered with thick feathers to protect them from the snow and cold of long winters.

Most owls hunt and move around in the darkness. In the daytime, they quietly hide in buildings, bushes, hollow trees, or on branches surrounded by thick greenery. The body feathers on most owls are shades of gray and brown to help them blend into the shadows of their hiding places.

For example, the feather pattern on an eastern or western screech owl looks like the scaly bark on a tree. When these small owls huddle next to a tree trunk, it is almost impossible to see them.

By hunting at night, owls avoid competing with daytime hunters such as hawks, falcons, and eagles. They also lessen their chances of being eaten by these hungry raptors.

In winter, when temperatures are cold, the eastern screech owl may snooze in the sunshine during the day to warm itself.

Long-eared owls normally hunt only at night, but they may hunt in the middle of the day.

It is not easy for birds to fly in darkness. To help owls fly at night they have very large eyes. The eyes of a great horned owl are the largest of any owl in North America, and as big as an adult human's eye. Large eyes produce a large picture on the back of the eyeball, and a large picture has more details in it than a small one.

Also, the pupil in an owl's eye is very big. The pupil is the black circle in the center of the eye. A large pupil lets more light into the eye than a small pupil does. It works in the same way that a large window lets more sunlight into a room than a small window.

Owls can also focus their eyes very quickly. This helps them to see branches clearly when they are flying swiftly through a forest at night.

Owls may also memorize the location and pattern of the trees in the forest where they live. Since an owl may hunt in the same forest for months, and sometimes years, it learns where it can fly safely so it does not bump into anything. Many nighttime forest owls also hunt in nearby fields and marshes where there are no trees to worry about.

Even if an owl can fly safely at night, it's an even bigger job to find and catch a tiny mouse on a dark forest floor. Animals that are active at night are called nocturnal (nok-TURN-ul). Nocturnal owls depend on their sensitive hearing, as well as their good eyesight, to locate and catch their meals.

Owls have better hearing than any other group of birds. The owls that hear the best are those that live where deep snow covers the ground in winter. These owls, such as the great gray, the northern saw-whet, and the boreal owl, rely on their sensitive ears to hear voles, lemmings, and mice running and squeaking underneath the snow. A great gray owl can hear a vole hidden under as much as 18 inches (46 centimeters) of snow!

Some people have claimed that nocturnal owls can see 100 times better than humans in the dark, and that they can hear much better than we can as well. This is not true. Recent scientific studies have proven that no owl hears as well as the average human. In fact, some humans hear better than owls.

However, owls see better than we do at night, but only 2 or 3 times better, not 100 times. Because we depend so much on lights to guide us at night we rarely have a chance to test our nocturnal vision.

If you were to go into a forest at night and sit for 40 minutes in the darkness, your eyes would slowly adjust to the dim light from the moon and the stars. In the end, surprisingly, you would see almost as well as an owl. Try it sometime!

# Owls
# FUNFACT:

**The snowy owl of the Arctic has the warmest coat of feathers of any bird of prey. It stays warm even when the temperature is −40 degrees Fahrenheit (−40 degrees Celcius).**

The long tail on the northern hawk owl allows it to make quick turns, which is helpful when it hunts birds.

In winter, many arctic snowy owls move to the Canadian prairies where they hunt in old wheat fields.

Although most owls in the United States and Canada are nocturnal, at least six species are diurnal (die-YER-nul), which means they hunt in the daytime, or crepuscular (krip-US-kyoo-ler), which means they hunt at dusk and dawn. The great gray owl, northern hawk owl, snowy owl and northern pygmy-owl are good examples of owls that are diurnal and crepuscular. All of them live in northern forests or the Arctic where the nights are very short in the summer.

Most owls use the perch-and-pounce style of hunting. They quietly sit on a branch, a ledge, or a telephone pole and wait for some careless animal to flutter, scurry, or squeak and then they swoop down on it. A hunting boreal owl may perch only 6 feet (1.8 meters) off the ground, watch and listen for two or three minutes, then fly to another perch and start again if there are no prey animals in the area. The owl may do this for many hours each night.

The soft feathers of a barred owl help it to fly quietly and catch mice even though mice have excellent hearing.

Some owls use other ways to catch their meals. The long-eared and short-eared owls hunt in open spaces, such as meadows and marshes, where they fly slowly back and forth, close to the ground. The great horned owl and the northern hawk owl sometimes flap-and-glide through open woods, hoping to frighten an animal and make it run from its hiding place.

Flying quietly is important if a hunting owl is to succeed. It needs to be quiet for two reasons. First, an owl always wants to attack by surprise. Any sound might warn the prey and give it time to escape. Second, noisy wings make it difficult for an owl to hear the faint sounds of its prey in the snow or grass.

If you open a car window while driving along the highway, you immediately notice the noise of the wind and how much more difficult it is to hear conversation. The noise is called turbulence (TER-bu-lence). To prevent turbulence when they fly, many owls have a fine feathery fringe along the front and rear edges of their wings. This muffles the noise of their flight. They also have soft fuzz on the surface of their wing feathers to prevent noise when the feathers rub against each other.

Owl wings are very large for the size of the bird and this also helps the birds to fly silently, especially when taking off. Compare this to the loud flapping of pigeons. These birds have small wings for their size, and their takeoffs are always noisy.

When a great horned owl is attacking prey, it never takes its eyes off the target. At the very last second the owl swings its legs forward to grab the prey.

This hungry snowy owl has caught a gray partridge, a common prey on its wintering grounds in the prairies.

The main diet for most owls is a simple one to remember: small mammals for breakfast, small mammals for lunch, and small mammals for dinner. Favorite mammals include mice, voles, lemmings, chipmunks, tree squirrels, pocket gophers, flying squirrels, pack rats, rabbits, and hares.

A family of snowy owls may feed on 2,600 lemmings in a summer. A hungry great gray owl may consume 1,400 voles in a year. And in its lifetime, an average barn owl may eat as many as 11,000 mice, whiskers and all!

Some of the smallest owls, including the tiny elf owl and the flammulated owl, hardly weigh more than a mouse themselves. These small owls are mainly insect hunters, preying on crickets, spiders, beetles, grasshoppers, and moths.

## Owls
# FUNFACT:

**The great horned owl is the most common owl in the United States and Canada, living in many different areas such as cypress swamps, northern spruce forests, deciduous forests, prairies, mountains, and deserts.**

Many owls hunt other birds when they get a chance. In winter, the northern hawk owl often hunts grouse and ptarmigan (TAR-mih-gun), and the fast-flying northern pygmy-owl attacks small songbirds such as juncos, redpolls, and chickadees. In New Jersey, a bold eastern screech owl once flew down the chimney of a house and ate the family's pet canary. It had pulled the unhappy bird through the bars of its cage!

Owls sometimes kill more prey than they can immediately eat. They store the surplus food for later. This is especially common for northern owls in winter. They may be unable to hunt for several days or a week because of blizzards. In these cases the stored food may freeze as hard as wood. Before a small boreal owl or northern saw-whet owl can eat its frozen meal, it must thaw it out. It does this by sitting on its food as if warming an egg.

When prey is plentiful, a northern hawk owl will often store extra food in the hollow ends of old branches and eat it later.

This burrowing owl has caught a meadow vole that is almost as big as itself. The bird is bringing food to its mate, which is nesting underground in the hole on the left.

Many owls also store extra food during the nesting season to help them feed their hungry chicks. They may store the extra food in a hollow tree, under a bush, in an old woodpecker hole, or in their own nest. One great horned owl nest in the Yukon had 12 uneaten snowshoe hares in it. Another horned owl nest in Saskatchewan contained 2 hares and 15 pocket gophers. Researchers who study animals are called biologists (bi-OL-uh-jists). They once examined a snowy owl nest in the Arctic with 26 lemmings stored around the edges.

Of all the owls, the barn owl stores the most for a rainy day. It often piles 30 to 50 voles, mice, and shrews around its nest. The record for a barn owl nest is 189 voles.

Snakes are an easy target for a hungry owl. Barred owls and several species of screech owls catch these reptiles when they can. The eastern screech owls in Texas hunt nine different kinds of snakes. Some great horned owls may attack fairly large snakes, even deadly rattlesnakes. One great horned owl in Florida tackled a 6-foot-long (2-meter-long) indigo snake. The owl won.

The eastern screech owl brings one kind of snake, the slender blindsnake, back to its nest alive! The owl does not eat the tiny snake but lets it go free inside the nest. The snake becomes the owl's housekeeper. It eats the worms, called maggots, that feed on the dead animals the owl stores in its nest.

Biologists were surprised to discover that baby screech owls sharing a nest with a live blindsnake are healthier than baby owls without a snake in their home. The researchers believe when there are many maggots in the nest they gobble up the stored food and the growing owls get less to eat. So the maggot-eating blindsnake is a helpful houseguest.

## Owls
# FUNFACT:

**Female owls are larger and stronger than the males. This may help them keep the eggs warm and defend the nest and chicks better.**

Scientists occasionally find a live blindsnake living peacefully in the nest of eastern screech owls.

The outstretched wings of a great gray owl can measure 5 feet (1.5 meters)!
With its wide wings and tail the bird can fly so slowly it almost seems to float.

Biologists know more about the diet of owls than they do about any other part of the birds' lives. The reason for this is simple: pellets. Once or twice a day an owl vomits up a pellet, or a wad of undigested food from its stomach. Owls often swallow their food whole and the pellets contain the leftovers from the bird's last meal that were difficult to digest. Pellets usually consist of small bones, teeth, claws, or insect parts stuck together with bits of fur or feathers.

The pellet of a barn owl is about 1.5 inches (3.8 centimeters) long and as thick as your thumb. Great horned owls regurgitate (re-GER-ji-tate) pellets 3 to 4 inches (7.6 to 10 centimeters) long, and a snowy owl pellet may be almost as big as a hotdog. By examining pellets, scientists can learn what an owl was eating.

Great horned owls that live in forests tend to be dark brown. Those that live in deserts and prairies are usually much lighter in color.

Spring is one of the best times to find and watch owls. This is when they hoot and holler a lot and are busy raising a family. Owls call the loudest and have the greatest number of calls of all birds of prey. The hoot of a great horned owl can be heard 2 to 3 miles (3.2 to 4.8 kilometers) away, and the hoot of a snowy owl, 7 miles (11.3 kilometers) away. Most owls have 6 or 7 different calls, but a long-eared owl has at least 12 different calls, and a barn owl has 15.

Most people think that all owls hoot. Some of the large owls, including the great horned, spotted, barred, and snowy owl, are good hooters. Others whistle or bark, scream and screech, chatter or toot.

## Owls
# FUNFACT:

**Large owls live longer than small owls. The barn owl, snowy, great gray, and great horned owls can live longer than 25 years. The boreal owl and tiny elf owl may live only 4 or 5 years.**

Barn owls are one of the owl species that do not hoot. Instead, they make ghostly screams. These large, whitish owls often nest in abandoned houses, old barns, and churches. It's easy to understand how a nervous person might hear screaming around one of these buildings and think the place was haunted by witches or goblins. If one of these pale-colored owls flew overhead in the moonlight, the person might think it was a ghost.

## Owls
## FUNFACT:

Small songbirds, crows, and jays often gather around a sitting owl and call out loudly. This gathering is called mobbing, and is a way for the birds to drive the dangerous owl away.

The barn owl is sometimes called the sweetheart owl because the feathers around its face are shaped like a heart.

Every owl has its own alarm call to scare away enemies and predators (PRED-uh-torz), which are other animals that eat owls. The most interesting of these calls is the one used by the burrowing owl. As its name suggests, the burrowing owl nests underground.

To keep predators from entering their burrow, adults and chicks make a harsh buzzing sound like that of an angry rattlesnake. Since rattlesnakes commonly use abandoned burrows as a place to hide, the owl's trick is a clever one.

The burrowing owl is a small owl, only 9 inches (23 centimeters) tall. It uses its long legs to run after grasshoppers and crickets.

Owls, especially chicks, also have a special call when they beg for food. It sounds like someone impolitely slurping soup.

The loudest call that an owl makes is normally the one it uses to advertise its territory. The loudest owls are usually males trying to attract a female partner and also frighten other males away. After a male and female get together, they use special, quiet calls to talk to each other when they are courting.

Once two owls mate, they must prepare to raise a family. They first need to find a nest. Most small- and medium-sized owls nest in hollow branches or tree trunks, or in old woodpecker holes. Here they are hidden from predators and sheltered from bad weather.

Several weeks before egg laying begins, a male northern pygmy-owl may show his mate several different nest cavities. She may squeeze inside each of them, or just peak through the entrance hole. In the end, the female chooses which nest the pair will use.

Old stick nests of hawks, ravens, and crows are favorite nest sites for larger owls such as the great horned, spotted, and great gray. Owls may use an old hawk nest several years in a row. They never fix it up or add anything to it, so the nest eventually falls apart and the pair must search for a new one.

The northern spotted owl is the most threatened owl in North America. It lives
in western forests, many of which have been cut down for lumber.

While the female burrowing owl warms her eggs underground,
her mate watches for danger above.

The burrowing owl is the only species of owl that nests underground, sometimes at the end of a tunnel 10 feet (3 meters) long. In Florida, these birds often dig their own burrow, but in the prairies they use old burrows dug by foxes, badgers, prairie dogs, skunks, or ground squirrels. These long-legged little owls like to nest in open spaces.

When prairie areas are scarce they move into cemeteries, empty fields, and golf courses, or along airport runways. At one golf course in Texas, a researcher found 27 golf balls inside an owl's burrow. The owl had collected the balls when they rolled near its burrow. Perhaps the bird thought they were eggs and it wanted a really big family!

Owls rarely add twigs, grass, or feathers to their nest. Burrowing owls are different. Many of them line their tunnel and nest chamber with dried bits of cattle or horse manure. Biologists think the birds do this to hide their own odor and fool predators such as red foxes, badgers, and long-tailed weasels looking for an easy meal. The manure may also attract dung beetles, which owls, especially chicks, like to eat. When a curious researcher stole the manure to see what would happen, the owls replaced the stinky stuff within two days.

Most owls lay 3 to 6 round, white eggs. The eggs of the tiny elf owl are smaller than a grape. Those of the great horned owl are the size of chicken eggs. When food is scarce, owls lay fewer eggs than when food is plentiful. Voles and lemmings are the main food of snowy and short-eared owls. When these rodents are plentiful, the owls may lay as many as 13 eggs. When the rodents are scarce, the hungry birds may not lay any eggs at all.

When a short-eared owl is threatened by a predator, the bird raises its ear tufts in alarm.

The top of a hollow tree stump is a popular nest site for the great gray owl.
It also uses the old stick nests of ravens and hawks.

All male owls treat their mates like a queen. Several weeks before the female begins to lay eggs, the male starts to hunt for her. He will catch everything she eats for the next several months. The female's job is to sit on the eggs and warm them, called incubation (ink-you-BAY-shun). In northern areas, she must cover the eggs most of the time to keep them warm because the cold weather would freeze them solid.

About five or six times each day, she may leave the eggs for a few minutes to poop, regurgitate a pellet, or preen her feathers. Even after the first chicks hatch, the mother owl stays with her young for one or two weeks to keep the chicks warm. During this time, the father owl hunts for the whole family.

Most birds begin to incubate after all of their eggs are laid. Owls, and many other birds of prey, are different. They begin to incubate after the first or second egg is laid. As a result, the early eggs develop sooner and hatch earlier. The first chick may hatch two weeks before the last one. The earlier chicks are bigger. They beg the loudest and get most of the food, so the smaller chicks often go hungry.

## Owls
# FUNFACT:

**It is rare for owls to feed on dead animals that they have not killed themselves. Dead animals, called carrion (CARE-ee-un), are readily eaten by other birds of prey, including hawks, eagles, and vultures.**

When hunting is good, there is plenty of food for the entire family. When it is poor, the smallest chicks may die of starvation. Dead baby owls are often eaten by their mother, or fed to the other chicks. When food is scarce, nothing is wasted.

Owl chicks are full-time eating machines! As they grow, so do their appetites. Often, by the time the oldest chick is two weeks old, the father owl can no longer catch enough food to feed his family. The mother owl then has to hunt as well.

## Owls
# FUNFACT:

Some winters when voles and lemmings are scarce in the north, owls such as the great gray, snowy, boreal, and northern hawk owls fly to southern Canada and the United States.

Even a large meadow vole is not too much for a great gray owl chick to swallow whole. The chick may swallow the rodent in just two gulps.

These barred owl chicks were born inside a hollow tree.

There's not much for young owls to do in a crowded nest while they wait to be fed by their parents. They nibble on twigs or bits of bark, and play with old feathers and pieces of fur. If they live in an open nest they watch the world around them: a red-tailed hawk circling overhead, a chickadee hopping along a branch, or a leaf floating to the forest floor. Young owls are called owlets. As they grow older they begin to exercise their legs and wings. They stretch, flap, and jump up and down. It will soon be time to leave the family nest.

## Owls
# FUNFACT:

Both the northern pygmy-owl and ferruginous (feh-ROO-juh-nus) pygmy-owl have two dark spots on the back of their head that look like eyes. These false eyes may fool predators into thinking that the owl is looking at them and prevent an attack.

Most owlets leave the nest when they are four to six weeks old. Some of the smaller owls, such as pygmy-owls, can fly when they leave, although not very well. The larger owls cannot fly at this age, but they can glide on the air currents and climb with their feet and beak.

It is important for owlets to leave the nest as soon as they are strong enough. When they are crowded together in one spot it is easy for a predator, such as a pine marten, black bear, or goshawk, to prey on the whole family. When the owlets leave the nest, they hide by themselves in different places, which makes them more difficult to find.

Even after the owlets leave the nest they are still offered meals by their parents for many more weeks. During this time, the young owls must learn to fly well. Sometimes they crash into bushes or land on a branch and end up hanging upside down.

Once they can fly, they must learn to hunt for themselves. They start with foods that are easy to catch, such as crickets, grasshoppers, and frogs. Later they hunt lizards, birds, and mammals.

Like all owls, northern saw-whets hatch at different times so the chicks vary in size.

The boreal owl is one of the most difficult owls for birdwatchers to see because it is small and hides in thick vegetation during the daytime.

Family life for most owls ends in late summer or early autumn. The owlets gradually spend more and more time alone, and their parents feed them less. One day, they finally leave the family territory and fly away. Some owlets settle close to their parents while others travel far away.

In Ohio, for example, biologists observed two barn owlets from the same family leaving home and heading in opposite directions. One went 600 miles (966 kilometers) north to New Hampshire and the other went 500 miles (805 kilometers) south to Georgia. A young snowy owl, however, holds the record for traveling the farthest from home. It hatched in the Canadian Arctic and ended up in eastern Russia, 5,300 miles (8,533 kilometers) away!

In winter, a dozen or more long-eared owls may roost together at night in the same tree.

A young owl faces many dangers when it leaves home. Some are killed by automobiles when they try to hunt in the grassy areas beside highways. Others fly into power lines and fences. Some are killed by other birds of prey such as eagles and hawks, and even more are killed by other owls.

Many big owls eat little owls. For example, the great horned owl includes eight different owl species in its diet.

The most common reason for the death of young owls, however, is starvation. The first year of life is the most difficult for owlets because they are not very good hunters yet. More than half of them die before their first birthday.

When hunting in the open, the northern hawk owl watches continuously for predators.

Today many people enjoy watching owls. For some birdwatchers, the great gray, the boreal, and the northern hawk owl are three of the birds they most want to see.

A hundred years ago, former president Theodore Roosevelt said people should wage war on the great horned owl because it killed ducks. Today, people think differently, and all owls are protected.

To see or hear an owl is a special treat, and one of the great rewards of nature.

# My BIRDS OF PREY Adventures

The date of my adventure: _____

The people who came with me: _____

_____

Where I went: _____

What birds of prey I saw:

_____        _____

_____        _____

_____        _____

_____        _____

The date of my adventure: _____

The people who came with me: _____

_____

Where I went: _____

What birds of prey I saw:

_____        _____

_____        _____

_____        _____

_____        _____

**140**

# My BIRDS OF PREY Adventures

The date of my adventure: _____

The people who came with me: _____

_____

Where I went: _____

What birds of prey I saw:

_____      _____

_____      _____

_____      _____

_____      _____

The date of my adventure: _____

The people who came with me: _____

_____

Where I went: _____

What birds of prey I saw:

_____      _____

_____      _____

_____      _____

_____      _____

*Explore the Fascinating World of . . .*

# Vultures

IN TIMES GONE BY, many people viewed vultures with respect and admiration. The ancient Egyptians worshipped vultures as gods. Mayan kings in Central America wore jewelry shaped like vultures, and Haida Indians in British Columbia carved vultures on their totem poles.

Worldwide, there are only 22 kinds, or species (SPEE-sees), of vultures. Compare this number with 222 different types of hawks and eagles, 61 kinds of falcons, and 212 kinds of owls. Even though there are not many kinds of vultures, the birds are very successful. There is at least one species of vulture on every continent, except Australia and Antarctica.

If you really love to watch vultures, the best place in the world to live is in Africa where there are 11 species. In the United States there are only 3 kinds of vultures: the turkey vulture, the American black vulture, and the California condor.

On a cool morning, the American black vulture can pull its neck feathers up to cover the back of its head to keep itself warm.

Several hundred turkey vultures and American black vultures may use the same overnight roost.

145

A Ruppell's griffon vulture lowers its legs as it is about to land near a carcass.

Biologists (bi-OL-uh-jists) are scientists who study animals. They divide vultures into two groups. One group is called Old World vultures. This group includes the 15 species of vultures that live in Africa, Europe, and Asia. The second group, called New World vultures, includes the 7 species that live in North America, Central America, and South America.

The two groups of vultures look alike and behave in the same way. All of them are large birds of prey (PRAY), which means they eat other animals.

One difference between the two groups is that they do not belong to the same scientific family. New World vultures are cousins of long-legged storks. Old World vultures are related to hawks and eagles.

Another difference is the kind of habitat they live in. Old World vultures live mainly in open areas such as grasslands and deserts. There are not many trees hiding the ground, so when the birds are flying overhead they can easily spot dead animals. New World vultures live mostly in tropical rain forests where there are many trees and where the ground is difficult, or impossible, to see.

In those habitats, three New World vultures—turkey vulture, lesser yellow-headed vulture, and greater yellow-headed vulture—have a special talent to help them locate food. They can smell well. This is something very few birds can do.

These vultures can find a dead animal on the forest floor just by following their noses, even when the carcass (KAR-cus) is hidden under grass and leaves!

None of the Old World vultures has a good nose. This explains why there are no vultures living in the tropical rain forests of Asia or Africa. The dense trees would prevent them from finding a meal.

Black-backed jackals and spotted hyenas often compete with vultures for a carcass.

Young king vultures are mostly brown. It takes four to five years for the birds to grow the beautiful plumage (PLOO-mij) of an adult.

It is easy for most people to recognize a vulture. Most vultures have no feathers on their head or neck, or only fine down feathers that resemble cotton wool. The reasons they look the way they do may surprise you.

## Vultures
# FUNFACT:

The people in the small town of Hinckley, Ohio, love vultures. Every spring they have a Buzzard Festival to celebrate the annual return of turkey vultures to their area.

Even without head feathers the birds are very colorful. A turkey vulture's head, for example, is bright red, and the Egyptian vulture in Africa has a lemon-yellow face and beak.

Other vultures are even more colorful. The white-headed vulture of Africa has a white cap, pink face, powder-blue jaws, and a red beak.

The most colorful vulture is the king vulture of Central America and South America. The skin on its neck is bright orange and yellow, its head is a mixture of purple and red, its eyes are white with a red ring around them, and it has some orange skin hanging from the base of its bill. Many wildlife artists think the colorful king vulture is more fun to paint than any other bird of prey.

The large flap of skin above the beak of the Andean condor is called a comb. It identifies the bird as an adult male. Adult females do not have a comb.

149

A vulture's bare head helps the bird in several ways. If a vulture becomes overheated because it has been sitting in the hot sun too long it can simply increase the blood going to its face. This gets rid of some body heat and cools the bird.

A vulture can also use the colors in its face to quickly tell other vultures what kind of mood it is in. For example, the facial colors of a hungry, excited vulture are usually much brighter than they are when the bird is calm. The same thing happens when people get angry and their face turns red.

Probably the most important benefit of having a naked head is that it helps the vulture keep clean. When vultures feed on carrion (CARE-ee-un), which are decaying animal bodies, their heads can become dirty and smeared with dried blood and rotting bits of flesh. With bare skin on its head it is easier for a vulture to wash and clean itself after eating than if its head were covered with feathers.

All vultures are big birds, and some of them are very big. Even small vultures, such as the turkey vulture, American black vulture, and hooded vulture, are three times heavier than the common American crow.

The largest vultures could eat two crows in one meal. Some of the biggest vultures are the Andean condor, the Eurasian black vulture, and the bearded vulture. All of these large vultures live high in the mountains in South America, Asia, and Africa. These birds can weigh more than 20 pounds (9 kilograms), which is the weight of a large Thanksgiving turkey.

The smallest vulture in North America is the American black vulture (top) with a wingspan of 4 feet 6 inches (1.4 meters). The turkey vulture (middle) has a wingspan of about 6 feet (1.8 meters). The largest vulture is the Andean condor (bottom) whose wingspan can be over 10 feet (3 meters).

Being a big bird has advantages. At a carcass, a big vulture can bully foxes, jackals, and other small animals, and take most of the food for itself. Also, a big bird can last longer between meals than a small bird can. Because dead animals are usually scarce and difficult to find, vultures must often wait many days between meals.

All vultures can go without eating for at least one week and still stay healthy. Some of the largest vultures can even go two weeks or more between meals. When they find food, however, all vultures stuff themselves. Because vultures are such big birds, they can gulp down three or four days' worth of food in a single meal. And they can do it in five minutes!

Lappet-faced vultures often proudly display themselves on a carcass.

The turkey vulture gets its name because its naked red head looks similar to the head of the common barnyard turkey.

Another good thing about vultures is the large size of their wings. The long, wide wings of the Andean condor of South America are the largest wings of any bird. The Andean condor has a distance from wingtip to wingtip, called the wingspan, of 10 feet (3 meters). A wandering albatross has a slightly longer wingspan, 11 feet (3.4 meters), but its wings are narrow and much smaller in total area than those of the condor.

## Vultures
# FUNFACT:

**The largest flying bird that ever lived on earth was a kind of vulture called a teratorn. It lived in South America during the Ice Age. It had a wingspan over 22 feet (6.7 meters), and weighed 175 pounds (79 kilograms)!**

No bird of prey uses the power of the wind better than vultures. They are masters at finding winds and using them to soar high into the sky.

One soaring Ruppell's griffon vulture in West Africa flew into a jet airliner at an altitude of 37,000 feet (11,000 meters)! That is about 7 miles (11 kilometers) high. The air temperature at that altitude is a very icy −50 degrees Fahrenheit (−45 degrees Celsius).

Vultures rarely flap their wings when they are flying. Most of them cannot flap for more than one or two minutes without becoming exhausted.

Vultures never waste energy flying like that. Instead, they depend almost completely on soaring when they fly. A vulture soars, or glides, easily. In fact, it is almost as easy for a vulture to soar as it is for it to stand quietly on the ground.

## Vultures FUNFACT:

The legs and feet of many New World vultures are black, pink, or red, but they look white when the birds squirt their liquid droppings on themselves to cool off.

It is not easy for a turkey vulture to take off for flight. Once in the air, its average speed may be 25 miles (40 kilometers) per hour.

The large feathers on the wingtips of the white-backed vulture give the bird forward speed. The rest of the wing area gives it lift.

Vultures are called scavengers (SKAV-en-jers) because they mostly live off dead animals. Sometimes lions, leopards, hyenas, bears, wolves, foxes, ravens, hawks, and eagles may also feed on dead animals. For these animals, scavenging is only a part-time job. For most vultures, however, scavenging is a full-time way of life. They do it better than any other group of birds or animals.

Vultures are good at scavenging for three important reasons. First, when they soar, they get a wide view of the land. Second, when they see a carcass they can get to it fast. Some vultures can glide downward at nearly 100 miles (161 kilometers) per hour. This is much faster than any running scavenger, such as a hyena or a fox.

The third reason vultures are good scavengers is that they hunt in the daytime. Many animals that die of disease, old age, or starvation, die at sunrise. This is usually the coldest time of the day or night and an animal that is very sick may become chilled at this time and die.

Vultures hunt during the day. This means they have the whole day to find the carcass and make a meal of it. The other scavengers hunt mainly at night. While they are snoozing during the day, vultures find many carcasses and pick them clean.

Many people think that vultures survive by cleaning up the scraps from kills made by lions, hyenas, and other meat-eating animals, or carnivores (KAR-nuh-vorz). This is not true. Although vultures often gather around carnivores that are feeding at a kill they actually get very little to eat from those carcasses. Vultures get most of their food from carcasses they find themselves.

Hunting vultures often search in groups. The birds spread out across the sky, each one searching a different area of the ground. When a bird sees a dead animal, it swoops down as fast as it can fly. If no other vulture is watching, it can feed on the carcass by itself, but this rarely happens. Vultures watch each other almost as much as they watch the ground.

Turkey vultures may feed on dead seabirds that the tide washed ashore the night before.

In East Africa, vultures are found in large numbers.
As many as 60 may arrive at a carcass in just five minutes.

When one vulture sees another vulture drop suddenly from the sky it immediately glides over to see what the cause was. This sends a signal to other birds nearby. Soon, there may be dozens of vultures soaring toward the carcass from miles (kilometers) around. As many as 36 American black vultures have been seen gathering at the carcass of a dead cow. Several hundred Eurasian griffon vultures may be attracted to a dead camel.

The largest groups of vultures are often seen in Africa. Researchers there once counted 250 Cape griffon vultures and over 1,000 white-backed vultures feeding on the bodies of 3 dead elephants that had been killed by poachers.

## Vultures
# FUNFACT:

**Vultures are the only birds of prey that commonly sleep together in large groups. In Florida, as many as 4,000 turkey vultures and American black vultures may sleep in the same clump of trees.**

A Ruppell's griffon has found a carcass and two lappet-faced vultures are fighting over which one gets to keep it.

Most vultures that live in the New World, especially the king vulture and the American black vulture, do not have a good sense of smell. Instead, they watch turkey vultures and yellow-headed vultures that do have a good sense of smell. Then they follow them and steal their food. Just three or four American black vultures or a single king vulture can easily bully a turkey vulture.

When vultures first arrive at a carcass they may not eat right away. The animal lying there might still be alive. A bird that is too eager to eat could be injured if it rushes in too soon. The hungriest birds are usually the least patient. Sometimes one or two of them may peck at an animal to see if it fights back. Often they will attack its eyes. If the animal does not move, then the birds that were waiting to see what would happen may suddenly rush onto the carcass.

While eating, most vultures fight with each other, shove, hiss, peck, and scratch. The fights, the noise, and the dust make feeding vultures more exciting to watch than any football or hockey game!

Because many vultures may try to feed at the same time, each bird eats as fast as it can. A lappet-faced vulture can stuff itself in 15 minutes. A Cape griffon can do the same in 5 minutes. The fastest feeder is the African white-backed vulture, which can tear off and gulp down about 3 pounds (more than 1 kilogram) of meat in 2 minutes flat.

## Vultures
# FUNFACT:

Vultures prefer carrion that is only one or two days old. They often eat rotting flesh that would make other animals sick. They can do this because they naturally have a very strong acid in their stomach that kills many dangerous bacteria.

Warm air helps birds soar. A lappet-faced vulture often must wait two or three hours after sunrise before the air is warm enough for it to soar easily.

The bulging pink crop on the king vulture is a signal to other vultures that the bird is full.

The birds do not actually swallow the food into their stomach right away. They store it in their throat in a stretchy sac, called a crop. When a vulture's crop is full you can see a big bulge at the base of its neck. It looks as if it has swallowed a grapefruit.

Usually, the skin covering the crop has no feathers on it and is often brightly colored. Andean condors have yellow skin covering their crop, king vultures have pink, and turkey vultures have red.

Biologists think that the colorful bulging crop is used as a clue to let other vultures know when a bird is full. A full bird is less likely to fight back when another vulture tries to push it out of the way at a carcass.

An African impala, which is approximately the size of a white-tailed deer, has about 85 pounds (38 kilograms) of meat on it. That is enough meat to feed 40 or 50 vultures. However, 200 of them may gather near a carcass for the meal, so most of them go hungry.

Many of the vultures that get nothing to eat are the ones that arrive late. The others are juvenile vultures that have not yet learned how to fight for their share. Even after there is nothing left to eat but skin and bones, some vultures remain for two or three hours. They may lie in the sun or clean and straighten their feathers. For young birds, carcasses may be an important place to learn and practice vulture behavior.

The heavy, strong claws on a turkey vulture are best designed for walking and grabbing, not killing.

Vultures do not have the strong grip and long, sharp claws called talons on their feet that eagles and hawks use to kill live prey. Even so, some Old World species and some New World species are able to kill prey with their tough feet and sharp beaks. In fact, the white-headed vulture of Africa often hunts and kills live animals this way, rather than search for dead ones. The white-headed vulture takes stranded catfish, and also attacks adult and young flamingos, baby gazelles, young ostriches, bat-eared fox pups, tortoises, hares, and lizards. These bold vultures may even attack a dangerous rock python or a puff adder, a deadly venomous snake.

Biologists have found that vultures eating termites is funny to watch. Sometimes during the African rainy season, dark clouds of flying termites fill the air and thousands more cover the ground. The insects are fat, juicy, and good to eat.

Once, scientists watched 70 lappet-faced vultures, 2 white-headed vultures, and 12 hooded vultures feeding on termites together. That day, these noble birds of prey did not look fierce or scary. The big birds behaved more like barnyard chickens chasing the tiny insects on the grass and picking them up one by one with their beaks!

When a hooded vulture is near a carcass, its flushed red face indicates that the bird is excited.

**171**

Turkey vultures may sun themselves together on a ledge. They can also watch for food below.

Although vultures are sometimes thought of as being dirty, this is not really true. All of them spend two to three hours each day nibbling and preening their feathers.

Every day many of them gather along sandy rivers, around desert waterholes, or next to mountain pools to wash. In Central America, researchers watched a dozen king vultures bathe together in a pool above a waterfall.

In Africa, as many as 100 white-backed vultures may gather and rest beside a river. Hours earlier, these same birds may have fed together at a carcass where they scratched and pecked each other wildly. At the river, they are quiet, peaceful, and friendly.

After bathing, they often stretch out their wings to warm and dry themselves. The birds may use the same washing areas day after day, sometimes for years.

Lappet-faced vultures display to each other during courtship.
It helps the female see which mate would be the best.

Vultures take a long time to mature. Turkey vultures and American black vultures do not find a partner until they are at least 3 years old. Egyptian vultures wait until they are 4 or 5. Condors, griffons, and lappet-faced vultures stay single until they are 6 or 7 years old. Once a vulture chooses a mate, however, the two usually stay together for life. Vultures may live 15 years or more.

Vulture courtship is not very exciting. Male vultures do not sing beautiful songs to their mate. They only hiss, snore, and grunt. They never bring the female gifts of food. They do not nibble on their mate's feathers in a gentle way. Male vultures don't even show off with fancy flying tricks. Some of the New World vultures may puff up their colorful necks and dance around a little, but vultures are generally quite dull when they are courting.

New World vultures and Old World vultures choose different places for their nests. All of the vultures in the Old World build nests of sticks, and they line the inside with dry grasses. Usually they build their nest in the top of a tree or on the ledge of a high cliff. Most of the nests are easy to see.

Some of the tree nests may be very large. The lappet-faced vultures probably build the largest ones. Their nests can be up to 6 feet (2 meters) across and 3 feet (1 meter) deep. They are strong enough for a person to stand in them.

In East Africa a white-headed vulture (left) and a white-backed vulture (right) may share a lookout perch.

175

New World vultures prefer their nests to be dark and hidden. Most of them are difficult to find. In fact, no researcher has ever found the nest of a greater yellow-headed vulture. Only about six king vulture nests have been found.

New World vultures commonly hide their nests in caves, in hollow trees, under tangles of vines or brush, or among piles of rocks. Turkey vultures in Canada often nest in the attic or upper floor of an old, abandoned farmhouse. The birds come and go through broken windows.

New World vultures do not build nests. They lay their eggs directly on the ground. Most vultures are shy when they are nesting and usually choose locations far from people who might disturb them.

## Vultures
## FUNFACT:

Vulture parents feed their chicks mouth-to-mouth. As soon as the hungry chick pecks at the parent's beak, the adult bird vomits up a hot meal from its bulging crop. The young bird takes the food directly from the back of the parent's mouth, or sometimes even reaches deep into its parent's throat.

African white-backed vutures gather dried grass to line the inside of their large nest.

The turkey vulture builds no nest. It lays its beautiful speckled eggs directly on the ground.

Vultures are like most large birds that live a long time. They lay very few eggs. All large vultures lay just one large white egg often marked with brown or rust spots, streaks, or speckles. If you made an omelet with the super-size egg of a lappet-faced vulture it would be the same size as one made with six chicken eggs. The three small vultures—turkey vulture, Egyptian vulture, and American black vulture—lay two eggs each. Their eggs are only one-third the size of a big vulture's eggs.

Hawks, eagles, falcons, and owls care for their young in a certain way. Once the female lays eggs, she gently sits on the nest and covers the eggs to keep them warm. This is called incubating (INK-you-bait-ing). The male hunts for the two of them.

When those chicks finally hatch, the female continues to stay in the nest. For several weeks after the eggs hatch, she huddles over the small, downy young to protect them and keep them warm. This behavior is called brooding. During this time, the father hunts for the whole family.

Only after the chicks are about half grown does the mother start hunting again to help the father feed their hungry, growing family.

Vulture parents, however, both take turns incubating, brooding, and feeding the chicks. While one parent warms the egg or chick, the other one hunts for meals. Every one or two days, they switch jobs.

## Vultures
# FUNFACT:

Some of the cliff-nesting vultures in the Old World, such as the Cape griffons and Ruppell's griffons, form large nesting colonies. In East Africa, one colony of Ruppell's vultures has 4,000 birds in it.

At about one month old, turkey vulture chicks are down-covered.
Feathers are just starting to grow on the wings.

The eggs of many falcons, owls, and hawks usually take about 30 days to hatch. Vulture eggs take longer. The eggs of the smaller vultures hatch in about 40 days, and those of the larger ones hatch in 55 days.

Vulture chicks never seem to leave home. Whereas young hawks and owls leave the family nest in about 4 to 6 weeks, many vulture chicks stay in the nest for 16 to 20 weeks. Even after they leave the family nest, many vulture chicks are fed by their parents for another 16 weeks. Some adult vultures feed their chick for almost one year!

One of the main reasons that vulture parents care for their chicks so long is that scavenging is a difficult thing to learn. Even with their parents' help, only 2 out of 10 young vultures live to be one year of age. Most die of starvation. Others fly into power lines or are killed on highways when they try to feed on road-killed animals. A few accidentally eat poison, and some are shot.

Biologists place colored tags on the wings of California condors
to identify the birds and to help them watch where the birds fly.

Twenty years ago, many vultures were in serious trouble. Today their future is a little brighter. For example, the California condor almost disappeared from the skies of the American West, and at one time there were only 22 birds left. Today there are over 200 condors. Nearly 100 of them are once again flying free in the skies of California, Arizona, and Baja, Mexico. The remainder are living and breeding in zoos.

In recent years, both American black vultures and turkey vultures in eastern Canada and the northeastern United States have moved north and expanded the area in which they live, called their range or territory. The birds are now more common than ever.

There is more good news from Europe and Africa where biologists and landowners have set up vulture "restaurants" to feed the local birds and help them survive. Vulture watching has even become a tourist attraction. Many people in southern Africa visit these vulture feeding stations to get a close look at these magnificent birds of prey.

All of this news is good, but there is also some bad news. In India, more than 95 percent of all the Indian white-backed vultures and long-billed griffons have died in the past 10 years. The reason for this was a big mystery that was solved only recently.

At first, researchers thought the cause of the birds' deaths was some kind of disease, insecticide, or poison. The reason turned out to be an unusual poison.

The vultures started dying after eating dead farm animals, something they had done in India for hundreds of years. The difference now was that many of the dead animals had been given an anti-fever drug just before they died. When the vultures ate the carcasses they were slowly poisoned by the drug.

The disappearing vultures in India have caused some unexpected and serious problems in that country. With no vultures cleaning up the dead animals in the countryside, the number of wild dogs has increased greatly, because there is more food for them to eat.

Wild dogs often carry a deadly disease called rabies. Dog bites from rabid dogs can kill people. Today in India, about 30,000 people die from rabies every year, and this number is expected to increase.

Indian white-backed vultures used to be very common.
Today they are very rare.

This example shows how humans are still connected to the other living things in the natural world. When one small part of this world is damaged or destroyed, humans may suffer because of it.

We must remember this lesson and use it to protect vultures and the other wild creatures in the natural world. If we do this, we may also protect ourselves.

Many turkey vultures spend the winter in Florida.

# My BIRDS OF PREY Adventures

The date of my adventure: _____

The people who came with me: _____

_____

Where I went: _____

What birds of prey I saw:

_____     _____

_____     _____

_____     _____

_____     _____

The date of my adventure: _____

The people who came with me: _____

_____

Where I went: _____

What birds of prey I saw:

_____     _____

_____     _____

_____     _____

# Internet Sites

You can find out more interesting information about birds of prey and lots of other wildlife by visiting these Internet sites.

www.adoptabird.org/ — Adopt-A-Bird

www.audubon.org — Audubon Society

www.peregrine-foundation.ca — Canadian Peregrine Foundation

www.kidsplanet.org — Defenders of Wildlife

www.animal.discovery.com — Animalplanet.com

www.EnchantedLearning.com — Disney Online

www.ggro.org/idhelp.html — Golden Gate Raptor Observatory

www.nationalgeographic.com/kids — National Geographic Society

www.nwf.org/kids — National Wildlife Federation

www.tnc.org — The Nature Conservancy

www.n-a-f-a.org — North American Falconers Association

www.pbs.org — PBS Online

www.peregrinefund.org — The Peregrine Fund

www.raptor.cvm.umn.edu/ — The Raptor Center at the University of Minnesota

http://endangered.fws.gov/kids/index.html — U.S. fish and Wildlife Service

www.kidsgowild.com — Wildlife Conservation Society

www.worldwildlife.org — World Wildlife Fund

# EAGLES Index

# FALCONS Index

# OWLS Index

# VULTURES Index

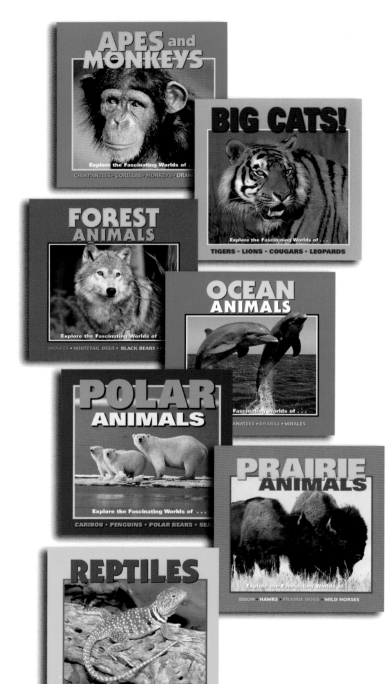

# Look for these Big Books in the Our Wild World Series:

## APES AND MONKEYS
ISBN 1-55971-863-3

## BIG CATS!
ISBN 1-55971-798-X

## FOREST ANIMALS
ISBN 1-55971-708-4

## OCEAN ANIMALS
ISBN 1-55971-781-5

## POLAR ANIMALS
ISBN 1-55971-832-3

## PRAIRIE ANIMALS
ISBN 1-55971-895-1

## REPTILES
ISBN 1-55971-880-3

NORTHWORD
Minnetonka, Minnesota